Game Tin..

Games to Promote
Social and Emotional Resilience
for Children aged 4 to 14

Robyn Hromek

P·CP
Paul Chapman
Publishing

Lucky Duck is more than a publishing house and training agency. George Robinson and Barbara Maines founded the company in the 1980s when they worked together as a head and as a psychologist, developing innovative strategies to support challenging students.

They have an international reputation for their work on bullying, self-esteem, emotional literacy and many other subjects of interest to the world of education.

George and Barbara have set up a regular news-spot on the website at http://www.luckyduck.co.uk/newsAndEvents/viewNewsItems and information about their training programmes can be found at www.insetdays.com

More details about Lucky Duck can be found at http://www.luckyduck.co.uk/

Visit the website for all our latest publications in our specialist topics

- Emotional Literacy
- Bullying
- Circle Time
- Asperger's Syndrome
- Self-esteem
- Positive Behaviour Management
- Anger Management
- Eating Disorders

ISBN: 1-4129-1072-2

 Published by Lucky Duck
Paul Chapman Publishing
A SAGE Publications Company
1 Oliver's Yard
55 City Road
London EC1Y 1SP

SAGE Publications, Inc.
2455 Teller Road
Thousand Oaks, California 91320

SAGE Publications India Pvt Ltd
B-42, Panchsheel Enclave
Post Box 4109
New Delhi 110 017

Commissioning Editor: George Robinson
Editorial Team: Mel Maines, Sarah Lynch, Wendy Ogden
Designer: Helen Weller

© Robyn Hromek 2005

All rights reserved. No part of this publication may be reproduced, stored in a retrieval system, or transmitted in any form, or by any means, electronic, mechanical, photocopying, recording or otherwise, without the prior, written permission of the publisher.

Rights to copy pages marked as handouts, certificates or overhead foils are extended to the purchaser of the publication for his/her use.

The right of the Author to be identified as Author of this work has been asserted by him/her in accordance with the Copyright, Design and Patents Act, 1988.

Contents

Introduction

Social oil and emotional resilience

Prosocial skills are the 'social oil' that makes getting on together that much easier. Social competence, emotional resilience and problem-solving skills are critical in a changing world that will rely increasingly on collaborative approaches to learning and dealing with problems in future workplaces. Effective early intervention is vital for children with skill deficits. Explicit instruction, modelling, guided practice and meaningful opportunities to try new skills are needed, with a bit of fun thrown in to motivate and facilitate learning. As the adults in a child's world act as teachers, mentors and emotional coaches, they build a supportive environment around them, increasing their chances of 'bouncing back' after crises or disadvantage. Playing therapeutic games with skilled game leaders provides tuition and meaningful practice of a range of responses upon which to draw in times of crisis. Children with a wide enough social network and a broad enough repertoire of skills can cope even when there are large gaps in some areas of their lives.

Therapeutic games

Therapeutic games provide a fun way of addressing socio-emotional needs while teaching practical ways of coping with crises and dilemmas. Besides being an excellent way to build rapport, playing the games allows discussion of social and emotional problems in a naturalistic way, allowing the exploration of coping strategies. A safe and supportive environment is created in which children learn and practise new skills. The games are structured to teach socio-emotional skills like anger management, teamwork, conflict resolution, cognitive behavioural strategies and communication to name a few. As well as being a useful teaching tool, the process of playing the games provides an immediate and meaningful way to intervene therapeutically.

This manual presents the theoretical background to this approach; the values, skills and attitudes needed by game leaders; application of the games; emotional coaching and emotional first-aid; and conducting a Life Space Interview (LSI).

About playing games...

I've been a game player for most of my life but owe the initial inspiration for therapeutic games to my own creative children. 'Little Friends' was a game made by one of my kids as an assignment for school. I immediately saw the value of the approach and have been making games ever since. From my experience, just about any therapeutic intervention can be turned into a game and become an interesting way for children to learn new skills. One of my favourite ways of working with children, especially with individuals, is to make a game together. The potential is there for the child to relax and learn while having fun. Games de-emphasise the 'talking therapies' without losing the value of what approaches like Cognitive Behaviour Therapy, Emotional Literacy, Resilience Training, Values Clarification and Desensitisation have to offer.

Children are often referred to educational psychologists and specialist support teachers for problems like aggression, lack of friendships, anger management, teasing, being teased, fights in the playground, etc. and establishing rapport can be quite tricky, especially if the child is oppositional and does not want the extra attention being provided. Using games can quickly disarm resistance, especially if the child is there with a small group of friends. Before they know it, they are having fun, talking about the issues and learning new skills. Whenever they see you, they will bug you to play 'that game' again. Teachers will wonder about how you are so popular with the kids. They will also wonder at the improvements in their behaviour.

Seriously though, playing therapeutic games with a skilled practitioner is a safe way for children to practise new skills. While they are having fun, they relax and discussion flows easier. Take time to familiarise yourself with the games. Start small and build up group size if you feel hesitant. Teaching points are embedded in the cards and on the boardfaces, making it easier to focus on the points that are most relevant to your group. Eventually you will feel comfortable with the scripts and teaching points. In conclusion, smile and have fun!

How to Use the CD-ROM

All the printable items for the games are on the CD-ROM in PDF format. You will need Acrobat version 4 or higher to view and print these files.

Depending on how you wish to print them, the games can be found in one of two folders: **Games for A3 printing** contains PDFs with the games on one page that can be printed on A3 paper or card (or taken to a local printer to print out and laminate), **Games for A4 printing** contains PDFs with the games split onto two A4 pages - you can print these out on A4 paper or card, trim and tape the two halves together to make the A3 games. We recommend you use a colour inkjet printer with photo-quality card to get the best results when printing these games.

The cards are in a folder called **Cards**. The first page of each set of cards is the colour reverse side for each sheet. Print from page 2 onwards then turn the paper or card over, reinsert into the printer and print page 1 onto the back of each sheet of cards.

Other elements, such as the decision cube, are in a folder called **Elements** and can be printed on A4 card.

The file directory on the CD is as follows:

Game Time Games

Cards	Elements	Games for A3 printing	Games for A4 printing
Calm Cards.pdf	Decision Cube.pdf	Friendly Friends.pdf	Friendly Friends (tiled).pdf
Face Cards.pdf	Little Friend Tokens.pdf	Friendly Island.pdf	Friendly Island (tiled).pdf
Family Challenge.pdf	Spinner.pdf	Give Me Strength.pdf	Give Me Strength (tiled).pdf
Friendship Challenge.pdf		Little Friends.pdf	Little Friends (tiled).pdf
Friendship Cards.pdf		Playground.pdf	Playground (tiled).pdf
Hint Cards.pdf		Roadrace.pdf	Roadrace (tiled).pdf
Money Cards.pdf		Strong and Smart.pdf	Strong and Smart (tiled).pdf
Physical Challenge.pdf		Tease.pdf	Tease (tiled).pdf
School Challenge.pdf		Think Again.pdf	Think Again (tiled).pdf
Smart Cards.pdf			
Social Dilemma Cards.pdf			
Strength Cards.pdf			
Strong Cards.pdf			
Tease Cards.pdf			
What If Cards.pdf			

The rules for each game can be printed from the file called **Rules.pdf**.

Chapter 1

Play and Socio-emotional Development

The importance of play

Play is the language of children and is crucial to their development. Children have a natural inclination to play and having fun is an important issue to them. The reciprocity between play and learning equips them for physical, social, cognitive and linguistic challenges (Smilansky & Shefatya 1990). Opportunities for language acquisition, communication development, hypothesis testing, problem-solving, behaviour rehearsal and the formation of mental constructs arise in the natural setting of a child's game. Prosocial skills like turn taking, explaining, negotiating, accommodating and sharing are exercised when two or more players are involved (Connolly et al, 1988). While engaged in play, children create 'scripts' that reflect the shared cognitive themes related to their cultural understanding (Fromberg, 1992). The helping professions use games, psychodrama, role-plays and simulations to develop insight and empathy (Dromi & Krampf, 1986; Porter, 1995; Sheridan et al, 1995). Malouff and Schutte (1998) field-tested therapeutic games by evaluating the types of therapeutic experiences produced in the games and the extent to which players enjoyed them. The results supported the effectiveness of therapeutic games with children, adolescents and adults. In a meta-analysis of moral education interventions, Schlaefli et al (1985) concluded that programmes that involved moral dilemma discussion and psychological development, ran for a course of 3 to 12 weeks and involved a supportive adult, produced significant results. Therapeutic games meet these criteria as well as being highly motivating for children.

According to the social cognitive theories of Bandura (1986), children's learning depends on their social milieu as much as their internal, inherited characteristics. By observing and imitating the interactions of those around them, children integrate behaviour into a framework of internal meaning. He concluded that programmes based on modelling, coaching, behavioural rehearsal and social reinforcement yield significant results. Vygotsky (1976), a child development theorist, postulated the importance of language as a mediating factor between a child and an event. He suggested adults help children develop higher level thinking skills through a process called 'mediated learning', that is, the process of guiding a child through learning experiences by using language to help create the thought concepts needed to meet challenges. Mediated learning experiences provide a range of resources a child might use to solve problem without explicitly telling them how to solve the problem. If one simply gives the solution to a child, an opportunity to develop higher level thinking skills is lost. By allowing the child to make associations between previous experiences and the resources around them, they learn important developmental skills. Words and language are 'resources' that can be used to surround events in a child's experience. They are symbols that assist in the formulation of the thought constructs that influence future responses. Therapeutic games provide a mediated learning experience of socio-emotional skills with a skilled game leader.

Therapeutic games

Therapeutic games are social interaction games that provide the opportunity to learn socio-emotional skills and enhance emotional resilience. While most children learn social skills from observing others or through explicit instruction, others have not learnt or do not apply prosocial skills and need extra teaching, practice and coaching. The natural inclination of children to play provides a highly motivating way to engage them in learning prosocial skills. Children are often referred for problems with aggression, lack of friendships, anger management and victimisation. Establishing rapport can be tricky, especially if a child is oppositional and does not appreciate the extra attention being provided. Games are highly motivating to children and can quickly disarm resistance, especially if the child is there with a small group of friends. Give them a dice and a few squares on a board and they will play with you for ages. Throw in some incentives and before they know it, they are having fun, talking about the issues raised in the game and practising new skills. While playing the games, conflict situations arise naturally, providing opportunities to model and teach prosocial skills. By using the strategies of a Life Space Interview (LSI), therapists, teachers, parents and carers can coach children through the crisis, helping them gain insights into their own and others' behaviours while learning the language of conflict resolution and empathy.

Playing therapeutic games with children has several advantages. Firstly, children are 'unguarded' when faced with the prospect of 'playing a game'. They are quickly engaged in a social situation that teaches skills while they are having fun. They are familiar with the elements of playing a game such as turn-taking, rule keeping, winning, losing and co-operating. Secondly, while children are actively engaged with the process of playing the games, social and emotional challenges emerge. 'Teachable moments' or crises occur, thus providing a meaningful and immediate learning experience. Thirdly, playing therapeutic games provides children with a safe environment in which to practise new skills. Children relax and discussion flows easily in this setting. Fourthly, clinical observations may be made and conclusions drawn about children who do not increase their use of prosocial skills after the extra tuition and guided practice provided. The presence of organic syndromes, mental health problems or child protection issues will need to be investigated.

The games progress in skill development and complexity with a strong focus on early intervention, ranging from ages 4 to 14. The games can be used sequentially over six to eight weeks or in one-off sessions to cover particular skills. Younger children would start with the 'Getting Along' games and work up to 'Friendly Friends' and maybe 'Think Again'. Children aged eight or nine and older would start with 'Friendly Friends', 'Tease' or 'Think Again', depending on the skill development required. The games can be used with individual, groups or whole classes of children. Topics addressed include:

▸ social skills

▸ friendships

▸ anger management

▸ coping with teasing

▸ cognitive behavioural training

▸ working as a group

▸ meeting challenges

▸ improving communication skills.

Social intelligence

Social intelligence refers to the ability to read other people in social situations and to engage and interact with them to reach common goals. For social interactions to be successful, we need a range of skills, for example:

▸ social skills – turn taking, talking, listening, sharing, greeting, politeness, apologising, paying compliments, seeking help, joining in

▸ friendships – understanding the difference between being friendly and being friends

▸ communication – receptive and expressive language, assertiveness, reflective listening, explaining

▸ problem-solving – conflict resolution, mediation, conciliation, negotiating, accommodation.

While playing therapeutic games, children learn the social skills basic to playing games together. They are asked to agree on some common rules before playing the games. The game leader models social skills and uses verbal reinformement to draw attention to children who are modelling prosocial skills.

Emotional intelligence

Emotional intelligence refers to the ability to read emotions in self and others and to manage these emotions so that cordial relationships develop. It includes motivation, zeal and persistence. When a game leader works with a targeted group of children over a number of weeks, it is possible to model and develop emotional literacy skills. Developing emotional intelligence involves:

▸ Emotional literacy – identifying where emotions are felt in the body, observing body cues, relating emotions to different experiences, words and thoughts, labeling emotions.

▸ Identifying emotions in others – observing body cues, words and actions, labeling emotion.

▸ Self regulation – using self-calming strategies, self talk, physical calming, problem-solving.

▸ Managing emotion in others – reflective listening, self-monitoring, clarifying, exploring, problem-solving.

▸ Healthy mind habits – thinking positively, organising, persisting.

▸ Coping strategies – perspective taking, seeking help, cognitive behavioural approaches, desensitisation, relaxation, fun.

Winning and losing

Issues of winning and losing need to be dealt with sensitively. Some players will get to the end of the game first, but winning is not the object of the game and should not be emphasised. Nevertheless, children are keenly interested in who finishes first or who has the most tokens at the end. Winning and losing are still prominent in the educational and social settings of most children and they will have to learn to deal with these issues at some time. The games provide an opportunity for leaders to acknowledge the bad feelings of not winning while using 'scripts' that suggest that it does not matter if you do not win. The main thing is to have fun while playing the games. Scripts or self talk give children alternative ways of dealing with not finishing first.

'Oh well, not everyone can finish first.'

'I'm glad my friend came first.'

'Maybe I'll finish first next time.'

'It doesn't matter if you don't finish first.'

'I had fun anyway.'

'It doesn't matter – it's only a game.'

Cheating

The approach taken to cheating will depend on the issues the leader wishes to focus on during the game, for example, taking turns and waiting patiently may be a focus for this game, therefore the leader may decide to overlook an incident of cheating unless someone else saw it happen too. If cheating is an important issue for the game, then a curious response is needed, for example:

▸ Ask, "How come you took two Little Friends?"

▸ Ask the group if they all would like to take two Little Friends from now on.

▸ Change the rules to fit the cheat.

▸ Ask questions about cheating and how others feel when someone cheats.

▸ Point out the consequences, for example, if we all take two Little Friends the game will be over too quickly.

▸ Talk about winning and losing again.

Chapter 2
Emotional Resilience

Game leaders may play a role in creating supportive environments for children who need extra help with social and emotional development. Emotional resilience refers to the internal and external adjustments we make when adapting to adversity and change. A protective social network for example, guards a child against victimisation, or the ill effects of a learning difficulty. Research into protective factors reveals a range of personal, family, peer and adult supports (Butler, 1997; Hawley & DeHaan, 1996; Walsh, 1996).

Personal or intrinsic factors include:

- pleasant temperament
- social intelligence
- sense of belonging
- sense of self-efficacy
- high intelligence
- a gift or talent
- work success as an adolescent.

Protective family factors include:

- at least one warm relationship with a parent or carer
- a sense of belonging and connection
- having qualities the family values.

Peer and adult support that is protective of children includes:

- positive early school experiences
- connection to school
- achievement of academic goals
- positive relationship with someone who believes in them.

Positive relationships with adults create a sense of belonging and a secure base from which children deal with the challenges of life. For some children from chaotic backgrounds, this role can only be filled by a teacher, or some other member of the community. Children benefit from long-term involvement with adults, helping to develop their sense of identity. Adults act as role models of the 'honourable self' children are developing. Social dilemmas can be used to clarify values and promote moral development and encourage their growth as responsible citizens of the world. Skills like social and emotional intelligence, academic success and habits of thinking can be taught to children to help them develop a positive sense of themselves. Teachers have a direct role to play in this process of 'skilling' children for the challenges they will meet throughout their lives. Blum (2000) emphasises the importance of actively creating opportunities for children to practise and develop leadership, mediation skills, decision-making, humanitarian activities, responsibilities, adventures, fun, recreation and recognition of achievements. Adults need to make sure they create opportunities for children to develop emotional resilience, for example, set up peer programmes, take a class on an adventure trip, clean up around your block, or visit a nursing home. Children develop emotional resilience when they have a network of supportive adults and a repertoire of adaptive personal skills to call upon.

Emotional coaches

For some children, emotional control is very tricky. Any perceived slight is met with furious, sometimes physical defence. Due to temperament and socio-environmental factors, these children need help when the flood of emotion happens. For reasons to do with the nurture of the child or inherited characteristics, a pattern of maladaptive responses is set up, most often aggressive but for some, withdrawal. Physiology kicks in and emotional first-aid is required. At this point, emotional coaches mediate between the child and the crisis. By applying emotional first-aid and following the steps of a Life Space Interview, (LSI) emotional coaches help children gain emotional control and then engage them in the problem-solving process. Issues like values, consequences, restitution and emotional control are addressed.

Emotional coaches come from a child's social environment and can be parents, teachers, aides, counsellors, headteachers, game leaders, in fact the more people acting as models for a child, the better the outcome. Coaches are emotionally intelligent adults who believe in the importance of relationships and are dependable, persistent and respectful role models in the child's world. An emotional coach has a repertoire of adaptive skills to model to children when dealing with emotion. They are aware of the emotional states of children and are skilled in noting physical and cognitive symptoms of emotional distress. They are also keenly aware of their own emotional states and know how to manage their feelings. They use strategies such as reflective listening and calming scripts to help children process emotion and apply emotional first-aid when needed. Coaches decide when a child is ready to engage in problem-solving by observing their physical and cognitive reactions and lead them in a non-judgemental and encouraging manner towards resolution and restitution.

In an emotional coaching programme, the coach and young person would meet for about half an hour once per week to talk about emotional control and identify functional coping mechanisms. They look for opportunities to model social and emotional skills while empathising with children's feelings and motives. They support the limits placed around their behaviour, allowing natural and logical consequences to occur. Coaches use a range of strategies, including the following:

- Teach about emotional first-aid – at a calm time, the body's physiological responses to anger are explained.
- Teach children to identify their body's early warning signals, for example, tight fists, chest, shoulders or throat, feelings in the stomach, legs or head.
- Determine 'fuse-length', i.e. how long between when they first feel anger in their bodies and when they are no longer able to think straight.
- Teach a range of anger management skills, including physical, thinking, communication and life style skills.
- Help identify the emotional control strategies that work for the child.
- Assist the child to set goals for emotional and behavioural control.
- Discuss what might happen if they fail to develop emotional control.
- Teach positive self talk that reflects 'calm' and 'control' and identifies the child's strengths.
- Create optimism through recognition of success – encourage persistence.
- Use the steps of a Life Space Interview when necessary – apply emotional first-aid, talk about what happened, identify feelings and values underlying the behaviour, talk about self-control strategies tried, give behaviour specific feed back.
- Review progress regularly, reset goals, reinforce success with rewards – awards, stickers, specific verbal praise.

‣ Work with parents, carers and teachers – inform them about the child's successes and the anger control strategies being used; obtain accurate feedback about how the child is doing in other settings.

Emotional first-aid

Emotional first-aid recognises that emotions are based on physiological reactions involving neuropeptides in the body. As such, they have a course to run, sometimes taking up to 20 minutes to dissipate. Emotional first-aid uses strategies that allow time and space for this calming process to occur while encouraging positive self talk and using reflective listening to engage the child.

Step 1. Assess the child's physical reponses

By observing the child's state, an assessment of emotional control may be made and steps taken to help stabilize their responses. When the following symptoms are observed, a calming response is needed until the child is calm enough to enter the problem-solving phase:

Physical symptoms	Cognitive symptoms
red, sweaty face	shouting
short breath	swearing
wide eyes, frowning looks	angry words
agitated and aggressive actions	irrational thinking

Step 2. Self-calming responses

Assist the child to apply a range of self-calming strategies, for example:

Physical responses

‣ Water helps cool the child while the time taken and physical exertion required help calm physiological responses.

‣ Taking a walk helps deal with the physiological response as well as allowing time to pass.

‣ Controlled, even breathing helps maintain the oxygen/carbon dioxide balance and reduce feelings of panic. Count 1, 2, 3, in - 1, 2, 3, out. The counts can change as long as the in and out breaths are equal. Counting breaths also has a meditative effect on thoughts.

‣ Some children need to be left alone for a while to calm themselves.

Cognitive scripts

‣ Calming self talk can help children settle. Use scripts such as 'Don't worry about it', 'Take it easy', 'Calm down'.

▸ Confident self talk can remind children that they can solve problems, for example, 'You can work this out', 'It will be OK'.

Reflective listening

▸ Say back the content of what the child says.

▸ Say what you think the child is feeling.

▸ Show that you understand the child's point of view.

Step 3. Use a Life Space Interview

As children calm down, they start to use more rational words to talk about their experience. Physical symptoms reduce and agitated activity calms down. By being keen observers, emotional coaches assess whether children have sufficient emotional control to engage in the steps of a LSI. At times during the interview it may be necessary again to apply the strategies of emotional first-aid as the child copes with the issues that are raised.

Chapter 3
The Life Space Interview

The Life Space Interview (LSI) is a verbal technique for working with children in crisis. LSI was developed by Fritz Redl and has been refined by Nicholas Long and associates (1991) at a psychoeducational facility in Washington DC. LSI is a therapeutic, verbal strategy that uses a child's reactions to conflict to expand their understanding of their behaviour and the responses of others. The adult or emotional coach assists in decoding the feelings behind actions and in identifying issues central to the conflict. Children are supported in problem-solving and in choosing alternative behaviours. By using reflective listening techniques, the facts are obtained, and values are explored. Therapeutic goals are established and consequences, restitution and future responses are addressed.

When children become emotional, it is often in response to some incursion into their sense of fairness and self concept. They may not have the skills to see the situation from the point of view of other children, but their own responses are often based on a firmly held sense of justice or fairness. By exploring these values with the child, coaches help them develop a sense of trust in adults who listen to them and see their point of view. When a child's values and motives are acknowledged, a sense of relief is experienced and they are in a better space psychologically to enter the problem-solving phase of the interview.

While playing therapeutic games, the LSI is best used as a brief intervention so the flow of the game is not greatly disrupted. Not every interpersonal crisis will require this level of intervention and the process can be shortened.

Basically the steps involve:

- identifying emotions
- offering emotional first-aid as required
- gathering facts
- identifying values
- identifying therapeutic goals
- exploring solutions and acts of restitution
- re-entering the game as quickly as possible.

The following scenario serves to demonstrate the use of a LSI to help children resolve a typical interpersonal conflict that might arise during a game.

Scenario

During a game, Mary hid the dice behind her back. John called her an idiot and Mary hit him in response.

Step 1

Assess the emotional state of the children. Apply emotional first-aid if needed. In this scenario, neither child was assessed to be overly distressed. Reflective listening and confident, calming scripts were used, for example, 'Looks like we have a problem to solve'. If either child seemed physically distressed, offers of emotional first-aid would be made, e.g. "Would you like a drink of water?"

Step 2

Focus on the incident. Gather facts, including the child's point of view. Use reflective listening to maintain rapport. From this step, it emerges that:

John called Mary an idiot for hiding the dice.

Mary hit John for calling her an idiot.

Step 3

Identify and empathise with the child's emotions. Use reflective listening to help dissipate emotion and help the child develop the language of emotion. Possible responses by the game leader include:

'John, you looked like you were frustrated when you called Mary that name.'

'Mary, you must have been feeling very angry to decide to hit John.'

Step 4

Identify the values behind the actions of John and Mary. This important step demonstrates a deeper level of understanding by the adult and releases the child from guilt, shame and punishment cycles of thinking.

Sharing: 'John, you wanted Mary to share the dice so the game could continue. Sharing and being fair are important to you.'

Fun: 'Mary, you hid the dice for fun. Having fun is important to you.'

Fairness: 'Was it fair Mary that you hid the dice?'

'Was it fair John that you used name-calling to solve this problem?'

'Was it fair Mary that you hit John to solve the problem?'

Step 5

Identify central issues and select therapeutic goals. Therapeutic Goal: to solve problems with words instead of name-calling or violence.

John used name-calling to deal with frustration.

Mary used physical aggression to deal with anger.

Step 6

Problem-solving phase – to create options for solutions and restitution. Explore alternatives to name-calling and violence. Help prepare the child to handle any consequence. Identify acts of restitution. Choose a solution.

What else could Mary have done to have fun?

What else could John have done to solve the problem?

Ask to move away from Mary.

Tell John you do not want him to call you an idiot.

Say sorry for hiding the dice, calling names, hitting.

Decide if it really matters.

Ask for help if you need it.

Step 7

Implement the solution and re-enter the game as soon as possible.

Importance of language

Careful use of language is important to help children take responsibility for their actions and develop empathy. Coaches and leaders model the language of emotion, conflict resolution, problem-solving and empathy. A respectful, curious approach is essential to the success of a LSI. For example,

▸ What made you decide to hit John just then?

This question suggests an element of choice and responsibility.

▸ What could you have tried instead of name-calling to make her stop annoying you?

This question takes a problem-solving approach to the conflict and avoids blaming.

▸ How do you think she feels when you call her an idiot?

This question encourages perspective taking and empathy development.

▸ What might solve this problem now?

This question is solution focused and implies confidence in the child's ability to solve the problem.

▸ You are really going to like it when you are the boss of your anger.

This statement is optimistic and looks forward to a time when the child will control their emotions.

▸ It will be great when you talk about your feelings instead of hurting people.

This statement is optimistic and suggests an alternative to aggression.

Chapter 4
Game Leaders

Skilled game leaders make sure a meaningful, therapeutic experience is provided. The skill of the game leader determines the quality of the experiential and therapeutic nature of the game. Game leaders with high emotional intelligence can build supportive environments around children through coaching and modelling skills and provide a deeper level of experience. The following skills and attitudes are important to the role of game leader:

Modelling prosocial skills

Leaders look for opportunities to model prosocial skills, for example, using manners, taking turns, saying sorry and resolving conflicts in friendly ways. Mimes, scripts and little role-plays are used to show children what standing assertively looks like, what adaptive self talk sounds like, how to seek help or what 'brag' means, for example. Leaders also look for and refer to peers who are using prosocial skills during the game. Smiling, having fun and being respectful are also modelled.

Using scripts

Language is central to the human experience, allowing communication with self and others, and guiding our construction of reality. There is reciprocity between the words we use and the attitudes we hold. Consider the following statements:

"I'm telling the teacher on you."

"I'm getting help from the teacher."

The first statement contains a reference to a social 'no-no' amongst children that may stifle help seeking and implies punishment or trouble. Using this statement may lead to the child being labelled a 'dobber' or 'tell-tale' and holds the stigma of 'being a baby' or not being able to cope. In the second statement the word 'help' contains the commonly accepted notion of helping those in need and the social acceptability of seeking help when it is needed. Even adults seek help from friends, or in extreme cases the police, if they are being harassed. When a child approaches a teacher with the words, 'Excuse me, I need help', they are more likely to elicit assistance from the teacher than when they say, 'Johnny's picking on me' in a whining voice.

While playing the games, leaders carefully choose language that reflects respect, calmness and confidence. Non-judgmental language encourages children to take responsibility for their actions and develop empathy for others. Scripts of adaptive self talk are also used by leaders to help children learn language patterns that will assist self-monitoring. Vygotsky (1962) observed that children's self talk or inner speech seemed to have a self-monitoring function. Scripts are samples of self talk to use when dealing with problems such as anger, frustration or conflict. Scripts allow children to learn and use new word patterns to form the basis of new thought constructs. Teaching scripts provides children with ideas and adaptive self talk to use in future problem-solving situations. Scripts should be simple and positive and reflect concepts such as control and calmness. Following are script samples which are presented as examples only and should be altered to fit local word usage:

- ▸ Oh well, not everyone can go first – I'll be first some other time.
- ▸ It's hard but I can wait for my turn.
- ▸ Don't worry about it, calm down, it's not worth getting upset about.
- ▸ What could we try to solve this problem?

Further script samples are provided with each game.

Verbal reinforcers

Specific positive comments made to children during the game are a powerful way to reinforce prosocial skills and build positive self-concepts. Verbal reinforcers need to be specific, immediate and applied liberally to be effective, for example:

- ▸ I like the way you kept trying to work out solutions.
- ▸ It's great that you waited for your turn even though it was hard.
- ▸ Good listening (waiting, sharing, helping, encouraging, comforting).
- ▸ Thank you for sharing (waiting, listening, being kind).
- ▸ That was a fair (kind, friendly) thing to do.
- ▸ I can see being fair (honest, helpful) is important to you.

Immediacy

Leaders constantly look for 'teachable moments'. When a child uses a prosocial skill that the leader wishes to reinforce in others, a verbal reinforcement is given immediately. When a player lands on a teaching point in the game, the leader draws attention to it through discussion. Likewise, when interpersonal conflict arises, the leader halts the game and leads the disputants through emotional control (as needed) and problem-solving processes. Leaders may wish to orchestrate 'mini crises' to create teachable moments, e.g., asking who wants to go first or who wants a particular counter. Almost every child will want to go first, thus creating a conflict between players. This gives the leader the opportunity to lead a problem-solving discussion about fair ways of deciding who goes first. Children will have a myriad of ideas of how to choose the first player. This negotiation opportunity would have been lost if the leader simply chose the first player. It also allows the leader to make scripted comments like, 'it doesn't matter if you don't go first', 'everyone gets a turn', 'I'll just wait for my turn'. Leaders may call upon children who did not care if they went first or not to explain why it didn't matter, thus providing peer models of alternative responses. Leaders should also surreptitiously stack the cards in order to direct the play – but don't get caught!

Discipline

Negotiate rules such as turn taking, talking quietly and listening to each other at the beginning of the game. Most are eager to play and will co-operate and encourage others to keep the rules. Model the rules, for example, waiting silently and patiently for children to listen after having asked them to listen. Suggesting that they will have to come back in the next break will motivate those who do not like giving up lunch breaks to solve problems. Use emotional coaching to help children work through crises. If the group is too unruly, stop the game saying, in a matter of fact manner, 'Let's try again next week'. Let the children know you would really like to play the game with them. Ask them what sorts of things would help make it easier to play the game next week. Reduce the group size and include a child with strong prosocial skills. This prosocial child's position could be rotated amongst the other children in the class who are keen to be included in a game.

Curious stance

An attitude of curiosity helps when dealing with crises. Being neutral, respectful, supportive and un-emotive will help establish a stress-free environment in which children can try out their new skills.

Awareness of reading skills

In order to avoid embarrassment, leaders need to help poor readers without drawing attention to their difficulties. It is good practice for the game leader to offer to read out all cards, strategies and concepts discovered during the game. Curiously, children will often insist on reading their own cards, even if they have trouble with reading. Some concepts will need explanation and discussion to ensure understanding.

Incentives

Every child player wins a prize. Children enjoy receiving something as simple as a sticker or an award or a lucky dip at the end of the game. This adds to the fun and motivation and ameliorates the pain of not finishing first.

Chapter 5

Using Therapeutic Games

The classroom

The games can be used in many different settings: in classrooms; with targeted groups; and therapeutically with individual children. At a classroom level, the games can be used to reinforce and support the teaching of socio-emotional skills through the curriculum. Most children are able to play these games by themselves after instruction, with minimal supervision. Parents, teacher's aides and older peers can also play the games with children as a way of teaching and practising anger management, dealing with teasing and friendships. By playing the games with children, adults learn a repertoire of skills to suggest to children, or use themselves. By teaching, we learn. The games can also be played as part of a playground programme where a passive games area is set up for students. Peer leaders are able to act as game leaders in these settings.

Caution: 'Tease' should be played with adults or very competent peer leaders.

Targeted groups

Social skill deficits that are not too serious usually respond to extra guided practice. Children with temper problems or who are involved in teasing or have difficulty making and keeping friends usually benefit from inclusion in a therapeutic games programme lead by psychologists, teachers, specialist behaviour teachers or teacher's aides. While the games are somewhat sequential, specific games are used to target particular skills. Playing the games at lunchtime as part of a whole-school response to playground problems is an effective strategy for selected children. With direct instruction, modelling and guided practice, most children will adopt at least some of the emotional management strategies presented to them. Most children identified to be at risk of social and emotional failure will respond to the intense, small group attention received while playing a course of games with a skilled game leader. By playing therapeutic games with a skilled game leader, children in need of further intervention can be identified.

Therapeutic games may also be used with small groups of children (four or five) who have significant social difficulties. In this setting, it is useful to seed the group with a child who has well developed social skills to act as a peer model. At this level of intervention, clinical observations are made and hypotheses formulated about the children's difficulties. If appropriate skills have not been gained after a period of instruction and guided practice, then other interventions should be initiated. Having played the games, one can confidently presume that children have been exposed to prosocial skills in an intensive and motivating manner. Further investigation of medical problems, mental health disorders, family dynamics or child protection issues may be required if progress is not made. Children who bully or are extremely disruptive or violent are not appropriate for this level of intervention but may benefit from the therapeutic/clinical level described below.

Clinical level

Therapeutic games may be used by educational and child psychologists with individual children who have significant social difficulties. Playing a therapeutic game with a child provides the opportunity to learn new skills without the distraction of others while quickly establishing rapport. The games provide many opportunities for therapists to raise relevant issues. When a child is confident in using the skills presented in the game, then other players may be introduced, gradually increasing the size of the group. LSI techniques are helpful when dealing with crises that arise. At this level, most children who have been victims of teasing and bullying, have poor emotional control or poor friendship skills gain at least one or two strategies to use. For those who do not respond to targeted or individual programmes, assessment and treatment by a clinical or child psychologist or a child psychiatrist may be required. An interagency case management approach with coordinated management strategies is needed and may include pharmacology, monitoring of social situations, parent training, social work, individual counselling, individual behaviour planning or special school placement.

Chapter 6
The Games

About the Games

Before starting work out some basic rules, like listening to each other, waiting for your turn, and saying nice things. If necessary, identify emotional first-aid strategies for those who get upset while playing. Cover the main teaching points as you explain the game and while playing. Make up 'scripts' or short sayings from the teaching points to use during the game.

During the games sprinkle liberally with verbal reinforcers like, 'Thank you for waiting' (sharing, using manners, telling us that, listening, sitting still etc.). Respectfully help children resolve conflict that arises. Hand out incentives or small prizes at the end of the game, eg, stickers, lollies, pipe-cleaners, plasticine, lucky dips, badges etc. Smile lots and have fun.

Preparing to Play

1. Equipment needed for playing the games:

   ▸ Board faces, instructions on how to play, rules, cards and novelties are all provided on disk.

   ▸ Dice – not provided, but a spinner can be printed from the disk. Print it on card, cut it out and push a cocktail stick through the centre.

   ▸ Counters – not provided

   ▸ Incentives – not provided.

2. See page 7 for printing and assembling instructions. Novelties include:

   ▸ 'Friends' for 'Little Friends' and 'Friendly Friends' – print about 30-40

   ▸ Awards for 'Playground'

   ▸ 'Pounds' for 'Tease' and 'Think Again' – print about 30-40.

3. Note that the same cards and novelties are used in several of the games:

   ▸ 'Friends' (paper doll images) are used in 'Little Friends' and 'Friendly Friends'

> ‣ ‘Friendship Cards’ are used in ‘Little Friends’, ‘Road Race’, ‘Friendly Island’ and ‘Friendly Friends’

> ‣ ‘Pounds’ are used in ‘Tease’ and ‘Think Again’

> ‣ ‘Calm Cards’ are used in ‘Think Again’ and ‘Playground’.

4. ‘Think Again’ has a Decision Cube template, which should be photocopied onto card, cut out and assembled. Kids love helping to do this. The alternative to the Decision Cube is to toss a coin. Heads means ‘Think Again’ and Tails means go to the Headteachers Office.

5. Keep a collection of incentives to hand out, like pipe cleaners, stickers, lollies, plasticine, cards, miniatures, dried apricots – any little things that children value.

Getting Along: Little Friends, Road Race, Friendly Island Lonely Island

These three games teach the language and skills of friendship to children aged 4 to 9 years old. Three boardfaces of increasing complexity teach basic boardgame skills while allowing discussion about friendly and unfriendly actions, thus expanding children's emotional vocabulary. During the game, children practise basic playing skills like turn taking, waiting, using manners, talking and listening, co-operation and dealing with winning and losing. Game leaders model friendly behaviours and social skills and respectfully help children resolve problems that arise.

Teaching points

Use the following teaching points as ‘scripts’ while playing:

1. We share special times and things with our friends, like hugs, secrets, toys, games.

2. There are lots of friendly things we can do with people who are not our friends, like share, help, play, cooperate, invite, join.

3. We are friendly and polite to everyone at school, even if they are not our friends – say thank you, please, excuse me, do you need help?

4. It's OK to get help if you are being teased or bullied – teachers, parents, friends, peer mediators, counsellors, principals will help.

5. Sometimes it doesn't feel good when you don't finish first but it doesn't matter – it's just a game.

6. Just because you turned over an unfriendly card doesn't mean you are unfriendly – it's just a game.

How to play

Play in groups of up to six children. When 'Friendship Cards' are turned over, leaders help read the words aloud as necessary. Players say what they think the word means. Answers are accepted and expanded through explanations, role-plays and asking others for their ideas. 'Stack the cards' to control the game, especially if a child seems distressed about turning over lots of unfriendly words (but don't get caught). Keep things balanced between talking about the concepts and playing the game.

> ‣ **Little Friends:** Players roll a dice, move the number of squares shown, and then turn over an 'Friendship Card'. If the card has a friendly word, players chose a 'Little Friend' token. If it is an unfriendly word, they try again next time.

> ‣ **Road Race:** First, players turn over an 'Friendship Card'. If it is a friendly word, players roll the dice and move the right number of spaces. If it is an unfriendly word, the player stays where they are. When players land on the Red Light, they miss a turn.

> ‣ **Friendly Island Lonely Island:** Players start in the middle. Roll the dice then turn over an 'Friendship Card'. If it is a friendly word, players move towards Friendly Island. If it is unfriendly, players move towards Lonely Island, according to the number on the dice.

Friendly Friends

'Friendly Friends' is a game about friendships designed for children between 5 and 12. Social dilemmas are presented for players to resolve. The concepts of friendship, friendliness, politeness and conflict are discussed. A key understanding is that children do not have to be friends with everyone but they are expected to be polite, and hopefully friendly. With this understanding, children tend to be more accepting of others and more likely to include them in games. Playing the game with children who exclude or are mean to others can be an effective way to encourage politeness, friendliness and kindness while outlining behaviour expectations. Include a child with good social skills in the game as a peer model. Game leaders model friendly skills and shape children's emerging skills while using problems that arise between players as 'teachable moments'. It is important that playing the game is not the only intervention used with socially isolated children.

Choose question cards suitable for the developmental stage of the players. Add your own for local flavour. Keep things balanced between talking and playing. Make up 'scripts' or short sayings from the following teaching points to use during the game:

Teaching points

1. There is a difference between being friends with someone and being friendly and polite.

2. We share special times and things with friends, like hugs, secrets, toys, games.

3. There are lots of friendly things we can do with people who are not our friends share, help, play, co-operate, invite, join, be kind.

4. We are polite and hopefully friendly to everyone at school, even if we don't like them – say 'thank you', 'please', 'excuse me'.

5. It is friendly to invite others to play with us, especially if they don't have many friends.

6. It's OK to get help if you are bullied – teachers, parents, friends, mediators, counsellors, principals will help.

7. It feels good when you come first in a game but it doesn't matter if you don't – it's just a game.

8. Just because you turned over an unfriendly card doesn't mean you are unfriendly – it's just a game.

How to play

Play in groups of up to six children. When players land on the Question Marks, a social dilemma card is read aloud and the player suggests a solution. 'Little Friend' tokens are given for friendly responses. All answers are accepted and expanded by asking other players for ideas. When players land on 'Friendship Card', a friendship card is turned over and a 'Little Friend' awarded for friendly words. The 'Share-a-Friend' square means a 'Little Friend' token is shared with the person on the left by placing it between the two players. When players land on the 'Rainbow Highway', they go to the end of the rainbow and choose either an Friendship Card or a Question.

Tease

'Tease' is designed to help the targets of teasing (7 to 14 years old) develop emotional resilience. The game must be played with a skilled game leader. Playing the game provides an opportunity to practise new skills while desensitizing children to the experience of teasing. The right to attend school without being teased is emphasised. During the game, children explore different responses, including things to say and/or do and identify a number of adults to approach when help is needed. An environment is created where players can discuss their feelings and thoughts about being teased. To help decide on the appropriate response to teasing, perpetrators are characterised as 'pests' or 'bullies'. 'Bullies' victimize others by saying or doing unpleasant things and usually do not stop unless adults intervene. Children should get help from an adult if they are being targeted by a bully. 'Pests' generally go along with a bully or are just silly and annoying kids who usually stop when asked. Children can decide whether to stand up for themselves or get help from an adult. Hint Cards suggest things to do including humorous sayings to lighten up the situation. The difference between being funny and being mean or sarcastic is explored. Children practise assertive responses while being careful not to make things worse. The game allows therapists to make diagnostic observations and devise further interventions where necessary. Game leaders model assertiveness, humour and confident language.

Important: playing 'Tease' does not replace the responsibility of the school for stopping teasing and or providing interventions for perpetrators. Tease should be played with a competent game leader.

Use Hint Cards to discuss different responses. Add teases that children have experienced to the Tease Card pack. Players must understand and agree to these two rules before starting:

▶ Do not take offence to the teases that are read out.

▶ Do not hurt anyone's feelings when you read out the teases.

Make up 'scripts' or short sayings from the following teaching points to use during the game:

1. This is just a game that lets us practise what to do if we are teased – remember to have fun and laugh.

2. Everyone has the right to come to school without being teased or bullied.

3. Just because someone says you are 'stupid' or 'weak' or a 'red-nosed rabbit' doesn't make it true.

4. When we say something back, being funny is OK – being mean or sarcastic will make things worse.

5. 'Pests' and 'bullies' are different and we can handle them in different ways.

6. We can stand up for ourselves when a 'pest' is annoying us.

7. Bullies do not usually stop when you ask them – get help from adults to make them stop.

8. It is OK to ask adults for help. Adults have the responsibility to make teasing and bullying stop.

9. There is a difference between standing up for ourselves and being aggressive.

10. Be polite to everyone at school, including 'pests' and 'bullies'.

How to play

Play in groups of up to six children. Include an emotionally resilient player as a peer model. Players start with £100 and a Hint Card and receive £50 for passing GO. Follow the directions on the board, including actions such as standing up straight and tall. Keep a balance between talking about the teaching points and playing the game.

Tease squares

Players pick a Tease and pass it to the person on the right to read aloud. The player chooses one of their Hint Cards to read aloud and is paid £50 by the Tease reader. If a player does not have a Hint Card, they think of their own response or buy a Hint Card from the board (£50).

Hint squares

Pick a Hint Card and read it aloud. Hints are kept until players are 'teased' in the game. When 'teased', players choose their best Hint, read it aloud, return it to the pack and receive £50 from the Tease reader.

Think Again

'Think Again' teaches children (6 to 14 years old) about managing anger and thinking before they act. Conflicts (What Ifs…) are read out for players to solve in friendly ways. A range of self-calming ideas are presented – talk sense to oneself, take time to calm down, have a drink of water, get help from adults. Teachers and parents should reinforce these skills. The difference between being assertive and being aggressive is explored. Tossing the Decision Cube (or a coin or spinning the spinner) allows exploration of consequences for aggressive solutions. Game leaders model respectful behaviour and teach 'scripts' of calm and solution-focused language to help children calm down and solve problems.

Use Calm cards to teach about anger management strategies. Choose 'What If' cards suitable to the age of the players – add some of your own. Make up 'scripts' or short sayings from the following teaching points to use during the game:

1. We all feel angry sometimes – it is not OK to hurt anyone.

2. We can catch anger early by listening to our bodies.

3. Stop when you first feel angry.

4. We can think about what to do when we feel angry.

5. Sometimes we need to take a break when we feel angry, like get a drink, take a walk, have a think.

6. Ask for time out if you need to.

7. We can stick up for ourselves by being assertive, not aggressive.

8. We can solve problems together when we calm down and take time to think.

9. Tell yourself you can calm down – you can work things out.

10. It's OK to ask for help when we need it.

How to play

Play in groups of up to six children. Include a player with good social skills as a peer model. Players start with £100 and a Calm Card and collect £50 for passing GO. Leaders read the cards aloud if necessary. When a player lands on 'What If', a card is read aloud and the Decision Cube, or a coin, is tossed (some games are provided with a spinner). When 'Think Again' (or Heads) is tossed, players think of a friendly way to solve the problem and receive £50. If 'Hit, Kick, Threaten' (or Tails) is tossed, players go to the Headteacher's Office, unless they have a Calm Card. Calm Cards are collected during the game to 'get out of trouble free'. Keep things balanced between talking and playing.

Playground

'Playground' is designed for children (7 to 13 years old) to address a range of issues from the playground – teasing, anger management and prosocial behaviour. The aim is to collect Awards from the playground (in the centre of the board) while keeping out of trouble. Players experience the consequences of unfriendly behaviour and collect Calm Cards with strategies for avoiding trouble. 'Playground' is a great game to play at the end of a series of games – or just for the fun of it.

Cover the main teaching points while explaining the game and looking at the Calm Cards and Awards. Make up 'scripts' or short sayings from the following to use during the game:

1. We all get angry sometimes but it is not OK to hurt anyone.

2. Stop and chill out when you first feel angry – take some deep breaths, walk away and get a drink.

3. It's OK to ask for help when we need it.

4. 'Pests' and 'bullies' are different and we handle them in different ways.

5. Ignore pests whenever you can.

6. We can stand up for ourselves when others are 'pests'.

7. We can get help from adults to stop bullies.

8. There is a difference between standing up for ourselves and being aggressive.

9. Being funny is OK – being mean will make things worse.

10. Be polite to everyone, including pests and bullies.

How to play

Play in groups of up to six children. Start on GO (the Playground Teacher), and move around the outside squares by rolling a dice. Players enter the playground (centre of the board) when they land on Entrance Squares with arrows. Calm Cards are collected to get out of 'Trouble' free. When players land on 'Trouble' squares, they move to whichever corner square they are sent to, unless they have a Calm Card. Players collect Awards as they land on them. Awards are read out and presented with congratulations and a hand shake. If player lands on an Award that has already been won, the Award is presented to the new winner with a handshake and congratulations. Keep things balanced between talking about the teaching points and playing the game.

Give Me Strength

'Give Me Strength' is a non-competitive game with wide appeal, including adults. The game includes fun and friendly actions like giving a compliment, waiting for others, talking about feelings, being kind and working together. Winning is not the object of the game and the game ends with everyone finishing together. Strength Cards have positive qualities written on them and are given to each other. There is a chance to talk about feelings when players land on Pick-A-Face squares. 'Give Me Strength' is a great game to play for group unity, or just for the fun of it.

Make up 'scripts' or short sayings to teach the following main from the following points:

1. Looking for strengths in each other encourages us.

2. Co-operation helps us get along together.

3. We are all strong in different ways.

4. Trust is important when we talk about our feelings.

5. Winning is not the most important thing in a game – trying our best and having fun are.

6. We can be kind to people who are not our friends and include them in our games.

How to play

Play the game in groups of more than three and up to six children. Players move around the board by rolling a dice and follow the instructions on the squares. Game leaders read out the 'Strength Cards' and 'Face Cards' if necessary. The game is over when everyone gets to the finish.

Strength Card

Pick a card, read it out and give it to someone who is like this.

Pick A Face

Pick up a Face Card and talk about a time when you felt like this.

All In Together

When a player lands on 'All In Together', everyone moves to that square.

Other squares

These squares include co-operative acts like swapping places with each other, allowing the last person to catch up, talking about acts of kindness and being strong.

Finish square

When players reach the Finish square, they can wait there for their friends or join the person coming last and continue in the game until everyone finishes together.

Strong and Smart

'Strong and Smart' is designed to help children (9 to 14 years old) consider the strengths they bring to solving problems. 'Challenges' deal with unfairness, hard work, restitution and cover school, peer, family and physical areas of life. Strong Cards explore values, emotional control and the importance of physical wellbeing. Smart Cards suggest helpful strategies like setting goals, positive self talk, getting organised, being persistent and focusing attention. The Australian Aboriginal story of the Rainbow Serpent is the inspiration for this game.

Cover the main teaching points while explaining the game and looking through the Strong and Smart cards. Choose Challenges suitable to the age of the players and add your own challenges. Make up 'scripts' or short sayings from the following teaching points to use during the game:

1. We can meet challenges when we stop and think about solving the problem.

2. We are strong when we stay calm, walk away from trouble, do our best, don't give in, keep fit and healthy.

3. We are smart when we decide if we can ignore something, ask to talk, tell ourselves to take it if we get out, tell someone to stop being unfair, say sorry, offer to fix our mistakes, ask for help, make a plan, concentrate.

4. It's strong and smart to say 'NO' to our friends if they have a bad idea.

5. It's strong and smart to say 'Stop it' if someone is being unfair to us.

How to play

Play in groups of up to six children. Players start on the Rainbow Serpent's head with a Challenge of their choice and move around the board by rolling the dice. Players collect Strong and Smart cards that meet their Challenge. Leaders read the cards aloud if necessary and ask if the idea will help meet the challenge. When players have both a Strong and Smart card that meets their Challenge, they call 'Challenge' and present their ideas. Strong and Smart cards are returned, Challenge cards kept and a new Challenge chosen. Not every card will meet every challenge. Players swap cards when someone lands on 'Swap'. Keep a balance between talking and playing the game.

Getting Along Games

Little Friends, Road Race, Friendly Island Lonely Island

These three games teach the language and skills of friendship to children aged 4 to 9 years old. Three boardfaces of increasing complexity teach basic board game skills while allowing discussion about friendly and unfriendly actions, thus expanding children's emotional vocabulary. During the game, children practise basic playing skills like turn taking, waiting, using manners, talking and listening, co-operation and dealing with winning and losing. Game leaders model friendly behaviours and social skills and respectfully help children resolve problems that arise.

Before starting

Work out some basic rules, like listening to each other, waiting for your turn, and saying nice things. If necessary, identify emotional first-aid strategies for anyone who gets upset while playing. Cover the main teaching points while explaining the game. Make up 'scripts' or short sayings from the following teaching points to use during the game:

1. We share special times and things with our friends, like hugs, secrets, toys, games.

2. There are lots of friendly things we can do with people who are not our friends, like share, help, play, co-operate, invite, join.

3. We are polite to everyone at school, even if they are not our friends – say thank you, please, excuse me, do you need help?

4. It's OK to get help if you are being teased or bullied – teachers, parents, friends, peer mediators, counsellors, headteachers will help.

5. Sometimes it doesn't feel good when you don't finish first but it doesn't matter – it's just a game.

6. Just because you turned over an unfriendly card doesn't mean you are unfriendly – it's just a game.

How to play

Play in groups of up to six children. When 'Friendship Cards' are turned over, leaders help read the words aloud as necessary. Players say what they think the word means. Answers are accepted and expanded through explanations, role-plays and asking others for their ideas. Stack the cards to control the game, especially if a child seems distressed about turning over lots of unfriendly words (but don't get caught). Keep things balanced between talking about the concepts and playing the game. Sprinkle liberally with verbal reinforcers like, 'Thank you for waiting' (sharing, using manners, telling us that, listening, sitting still). Hand out incentives or small prizes at the end of the game, for example, stickers, lollies, pipe-cleaners, plasticine, lucky dips, badges. Smile lots and have fun.

▸ **Little Friends:** Players roll a dice, move the number of squares shown, then turn over an 'Friendship Card'. If the card has a friendly word, players chose a 'Little Friend' token. If it is an unfriendly word, they try again next time.

▸ **Road Race:** First, players turn over an 'Friendship Card'. If it is a friendly word, players roll the dice and move the right number of spaces. If it is an unfriendly word, the player stays where they are. When players land on the Red Light, they miss a turn.

▸ **Friendly Island Lonely Island:** Players start in the middle. Roll the dice then turn over a 'Friendship Card'. If it is a friendly word, players move towards Friendly Island. If it is unfriendly, players move towards Lonely Island, according to the number on the dice.

Little Friends

Equipment

- Game Board (CD)
- Little Friends (CD)
- Dice or spinner (CD)
- Friendship Cards (CD)
- Counters
- Incentives

Rules

The aim is to win as many Little Friends as you can.

- Decide who is going first.
- Roll the dice, move around the board and then turn over a Friendship card.
- If it is a friendly word choose a Little Friend.

  Explain any words that might be hard to understand.

  Discuss the words turned over, for example, what is something kind we can do?

- Continue until everyone reaches the FINISH.

Have Fun!

Road Race

Equipment

- Game Board (CD)
- Friendship Cards (CD)
- Counters
- Dice or Spinner (CD)
- Incentives

Rules

The aim is to get to the FINISH as quickly as you can.

- Decide who is going first.

- Turn over a Friendship Card.

- If it is a friendly word roll the dice and move forward the number of spaces shown.

- If it is an unfriendly word, stay where you are.

- Miss a turn if you land on the RED LIGHT.

  Explain any words that might be hard to understand.

  Discuss the words turned over, for example, what is something kind we can do?

- Continue until everyone reaches the FINISH.

Have Fun!

Friendly Island Lonely Island

Equipment

- Game Board (CD)
- Friendship Cards (CD)
- Counters
- Dice or Spinner (CD)
- Incentives

Rules

The aim is to get to Friendly Island as quickly as you can.

- Start in the middle.

- Roll the dice and turn over a Friendship Card.

- If it is a friendly word, move towards Friendly Island.

- If it is an unfriendly word, move towards Lonely Island.

  Explain any hard words. Talk about the words turned over eg, what is something kind we can do?

- Continue until everyone reaches Friendly Island.

Have Fun!

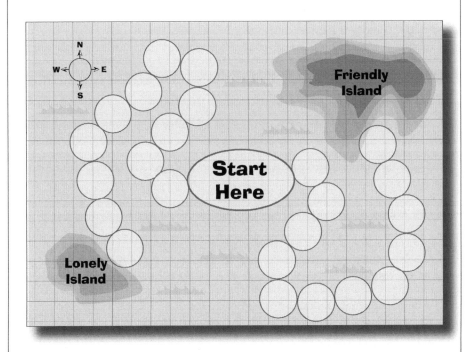

Friendship Skills

Friendly Friends

'Friendly Friends' is a game about friendships designed for children aged between 5 and 12. Social dilemmas are presented for players to resolve. The concepts of friendship, friendliness, politeness and conflict are discussed. A key understanding is that children do not have to be friends with everyone but they are expected to be polite, and hopefully friendly. With this understanding, children tend to be more accepting of others and more likely to include them in games. Playing the game with children who exclude or are mean to others can be an effective way to encourage politeness, friendliness and kindness while outlining behaviour expectations. Include a child with good social skills in the game as a peer model. Game leaders model friendly skills and shape children's emerging skills while using problems that arise between players as 'teachable moments'. It is important that playing the game is not the only intervention used with socially isolated children.

Before starting

Work out some basic rules, like listening to each other, waiting for your turn, and saying nice things. If necessary, identify emotional first-aid strategies for anyone who gets upset while playing. Cover the main teaching points while explaining the game. Choose question cards suitable for the developmental stage of the players. Keep things balanced between talking and playing. Make up 'scripts' or short sayings from the following teaching points to use during the game:

1. There is a difference between being friends with someone and being friendly and polite.

2. We share special times and things with friends, like hugs, secrets, toys, games.

3. There are lots of friendly things we can do with people who are not our friends – share, help, play, co-operate, invite, join, be kind.

4. We are polite to everyone at school, even if we don't like them – say 'thank you', 'please', 'excuse me'.

5. It is friendly to invite others to play with us, especially if they don't have many friends.

6. It's OK to get help if you are bullied – teachers, parents, friends, mediators, counsellors, headteachers will help.

7. It feels good when you come first in a game but it doesn't matter if you don't – it's just a game.

8. Just because you turned over an unfriendly card doesn't mean you are unfriendly – it's just a game.

How the game works

Play in small groups of up to six children. When players land on the Question Marks, a social dilemma card is read aloud and the player suggests a solution. 'Little Friend' tokens are given for friendly responses. All answers are accepted and expanded by asking other players for ideas. When players land on 'Friendship Card', a friendship card is turned over and a 'Little Friend' awarded for friendly words. The 'Share-a-Friend' square means a 'Little Friend' token is shared with the person on the left by placing it between the two players. When players land on the 'Rainbow Highway', they go to the end of the rainbow. Sprinkle liberally with verbal reinforcers, for example, 'Thank you for waiting' (sharing, using manners, telling us that). Respectfully help children resolve any problems that arise. Hand out incentives or small 'prizes' at the end, for example, stickers, lollies, pipe-cleaners, plasticine, lucky dips, badges, pens. Smile lots and have fun.

Friendly Friends

Equipment

- ▸ Game Board (CD)
- ▸ Social Dilemma Cards (CD)
- ▸ Counters
- ▸ Incentives

- ▸ Friendship Cards (CD)
- ▸ Little Friends (CD)
- ▸ Dice or Spinner (CD)

Rules

The aim is to win as many FRIENDS as you can while solving problems in friendly ways.

Squares

- ▸ **Friendship Cards:** Turn over a Friendship Card and read the word aloud. If it is friendly, pick up a FRIEND token.

- ▸ **Questions:** Pick a question, read it aloud and suggest a solution. If the answer is friendly, pick up a FRIEND token.

- ▸ **Rainbow Highway:** If you land on the Rainbow Highway, go to the end of the Rainbow and choose a question or a Friendship Card.

- ▸ Talk about the meanings of the words and the problems.

- ▸ Continue until all the friends are won.

Have Fun!

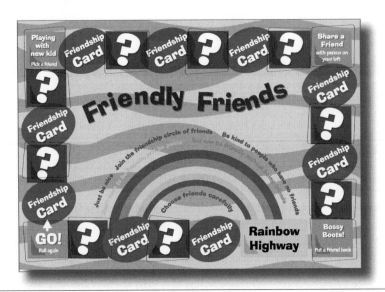

Resilience Training

Tease

'Tease' is designed to help targets of teasing aged 7 to 14 develop emotional resilience and must be played with a skilled game leader. Playing the game provides an opportunity to practise new skills while desensitizing children to the experience of teasing. The right to attend school without being teased is emphasised. During the game, children identify adults to approach if help is needed and explore different responses, including things to say and do. An environment is created where players can discuss their feelings and thoughts about being teased. To help decide on the appropriate response to teasing, perpetrators are characterised as 'pests' or 'bullies'. 'Bullies' victimize others by saying or doing unpleasant things and usually do not stop unless adults intervene. Children should get help from an adult if they are being targeted by a bully. 'Pests' generally go along with a bully or are just silly and annoying kids who usually stop when asked. Children can decide whether to stand up for themselves or get help from an adult. Hint Cards suggest things to do including humorous sayings to lighten up the situation. The difference between being funny and being mean or sarcastic is explored. Children practise being assertive without making things worse. The game allows adults to make observations and devise further interventions where necessary. Game leaders model assertiveness, humour and confident language.

Important: playing 'Tease' does not replace the responsibility of the school for stopping teasing and for providing support for all involved.

Before starting

Work out some basic rules, like listening, waiting, and saying nice things. If necessary, identify emotional first-aid strategies for anyone who gets upset while playing. Cover the main teaching points while explaining the game. Use Hint Cards to discuss different responses. Add teases that children have experienced to the Tease Card pack. Players must understand and agree to these two rules before starting:

  ▶ Do not take offence to the teases that are read out.

  ▶ Do not hurt anyone's feelings when you read out the teases.

Make up 'scripts' or short sayings from the following teaching points to use during the game:

1. This is just a game that lets us practise what to do if we are teased – remember to have fun and laugh.

2. Everyone has the right to come to school without being teased or bullied.

3. Just because someone says you are 'stupid' or 'weak' or a 'red-nosed rabbit' doesn't make it true.

4. When we say something back, being funny is OK – being mean or sarcastic will make things worse.

5. 'Pests' and 'bullies' are different and we can handle them in different ways.

6. We can stand up for ourselves when a 'pest' is annoying us.

7. Bullies do not usually stop when you ask them – get help from adults to make them stop.

8. It is OK to ask adults for help. Adults have the responsibility to make teasing and bullying stop.

9. There is a difference between standing up for ourselves and being aggressive.

10. Be polite to everyone at school, including 'pests' and 'bullies'.

How the game works

Play in groups of up to six children. Include an emotionally resilient player as a peer model. Players start with £100 and a Hint Card and receive £50 for passing GO. Follow the directions on the board, including actions such as standing up straight and tall. Keep a balance between talking about the teaching points and playing the game. Sprinkle liberally with verbal reinforcers, for example, 'Thank you for waiting' (sharing, using manners, telling us that). Respectfully help children resolve any problems that arise. Hand out incentives or small 'prizes' at the end, for example, stickers, lollies, pipe-cleaners, plasticine, lucky dips, badges, pens. Smile lots and have fun.

Tease squares: Players pick a Tease and pass it to the person on the right to read aloud. The player chooses one of their Hint Cards to read aloud and is paid £50 by the Tease reader. If a player does not have a Hint Card, they think of their own response or buy a Hint Card from the board (£50).

Hint squares: Pick a Hint Card and read it aloud. Hints are kept until players are 'Teased' in the game. When 'Teased', players choose their best Hint, read it aloud, return it to the pack and receive £50 from the Tease reader.

Tease

Equipment

- Game Board (CD)
- Tease Cards (CD)
- Hint Cards (CD)
- Play Money (CD)
- Counters
- Dice or Spinner (CD)
- Incentives

Rules

The aim is to collect as much money as you can while collecting Hints for responding to the Teases. Start on GO with £100 and a Hint. Move around the board by rolling a dice. Talk about whether the ideas on the Hint Cards would work for pests or bullies.

Important: Do not let your feelings get hurt. Do not hurt anyone's feelings.

It's only a game that lets us practise what to do if we are teased.

Squares

- **Tease Cards:** Hand the Tease Card to the person on the right. After they read the Tease aloud, choose a response from your Hint Cards and receive £50 from the Tease reader.

- **Hint Cards:** Read the Hint aloud and keep it. When you are 'teased', choose your best Hint, read it aloud and return it to the pack. If you don't have a Hint, think of something you could do or buy a Hint for £50.

- **Pests and bullies:** Talk about the difference between a pest and a bully. A pest is annoying but will usually stop when asked. A bully is very mean and won't usually stop unless an adult helps.

- **Stay calm:** Talk about the kinds of things that help you stay calm, for example, taking a deep breath, walking away to have a drink, thinking.

- **Stand confidently:** Show how you stand up tall around pests and bullies.

- **Getting help:** Tell who you would ask to help you if you were being bullied.

Continue until you are out of time or money.

Have Fun!

Anger Management

Think Again

'Think Again' teaches children aged 6 to 14 about managing anger and thinking before they act. Conflicts are read out for players to solve in friendly ways. A range of self-calming ideas are presented – talk sense to oneself, take time to calm down, have a drink of water, get help from adults. Teachers and parents should reinforce these skills. The difference between being assertive and being aggressive is explored. Tossing the Decision Cube allows consequences for aggressive solutions. Game leaders model respectful behaviour and teach 'scripts' of calm and solution-focused language to help children calm down and solve problems.

Before starting

Work out some basic rules, like listening to each other, waiting for your turn, and saying nice things. If necessary, identify emotional first-aid strategies for anyone who gets upset while playing. Cover the main teaching points while explaining the game. Use Calm cards to teach about anger management strategies. Choose 'What If' cards suitable to the age of the players – add some of your own. Make up 'scripts' or short sayings from the following teaching points to use during the game:

1. We all feel angry sometimes – it is not OK to hurt anyone.

2. We can catch anger early by listening to our bodies.

3. Stop when you first feel angry.

4. We can think about what to do when we feel angry.

5. Sometimes we need to take a break when we feel angry, like get a drink, take a walk, have a think.

6. Ask for time out if you need to.

7. We can stick up for ourselves by being assertive, not aggressive.

8. We can solve problems together when we calm down and take time to think.

9. Tell yourself you can calm down – you can work things out.

10. It's OK to ask for help when we need it.

How to play the game

Play in groups of up to six children. Include a player with good social skills as a peer model. Players start with £100 and a Calm Card and collect £50 for passing GO. Leaders read the cards aloud if necessary. When a player lands on 'What If', a card is read aloud and the Decision Cube (alternatively, a coin) is tossed. When 'Think Again' (or Heads) is tossed, players think of a friendly way to solve the problem and receive £50. If 'Hit, Kick, Threaten' (or Tails) is tossed, players go to the Headteacher's Office, unless they have a Calm Card. Calm Cards are collected during the game to 'get out of trouble free'. Keep things balanced between talking and playing. Sprinkle liberally with verbal reinforcers like, 'Thank you for waiting' (sharing, using manners, telling us that, listening). Respectfully help children resolve any problems that arise. Hand out small prizes at the end of the game, for example, stickers, lollies, pipe-cleaners, plasticine, lucky dips, badges. Smile lots and have fun.

Think Again

Equipment

- ▸ Game Board (CD)
- ▸ What If... Cards (CD)
- ▸ Calm Cards (CD)
- ▸ Decision Cube (or a coin) (CD)
- ▸ Play Money (CD)
- ▸ Dice or Spinner (CD)
- ▸ Counters
- ▸ Incentives

Rules

The aim is to collect as much money as you can while keeping out of trouble and solving problems. Start on GO with £100 and a Calm Card.

Decision Cube (or coin): If the cube lands on Think Again (or coin on Heads), think of a friendly way to solve the problem and collect £50. If the cube lands on 'kick fight bite hit swear threaten' (or coin on Tails), go to the Headteacher's Office – unless you have a Calm Card.

Squares

What if...: Read the What If card aloud. Roll the decision cube (or toss a coin) and follow the instructions.

Calm Cards: Read the Calm Card aloud and keep it to get out of the Headteacher's Office free. Return the Calm Card to the pack after use.

Headteacher's Office: Move to this square if the cube (or coin) has sent you there. Get out by rolling a 6 or paying £50 or by handing in a Calm Card. Visitors roll again.

Suspended: Miss a turn.

Other squares: Follow the directions on the board and talk about the issues.

Continue until you are out of time or money.

Have Fun!

Playground Issues

Playground

'Playground' is designed for children aged 7 to 13 to address a range of issues from the playground – teasing, anger management and prosocial behaviour. The aim is to collect Awards from the playground (in the centre of the board) while keeping out of trouble. Players experience the consequences of unfriendly behaviour and collect Calm Cards with strategies for avoiding trouble. 'Playground' is a great game to play at the end of a series of games as well as just for the fun of it.

Before starting

Work out some basic rules, like listening to each other, waiting for your turn, and saying nice things to each other. If necessary, identify emotional first-aid strategies for anyone who gets upset while playing. Cover the main teaching points while explaining the game and looking at the Calm Cards and Awards. Make up 'scripts' or short sayings from the following to use during the game:

1. We all get angry sometimes but it is not OK to hurt anyone.

2. Stop and chill out when you first feel angry – take some deep breaths, walk away and get a drink.

3. It's OK to ask for help when we need it.

4. 'Pests' and 'bullies' are different and we handle them in different ways.

5. Ignore pests whenever you can.

6. We can stand up for ourselves when others are 'pests'.

7. We can get help from adults to stop bullies.

8. There is a difference between standing up for ourselves and being aggressive.

9. Being funny is OK – being mean will make things worse.

10. Be polite to everyone, including pests and bullies.

How the game works

Play in groups of up to six children. Start on GO, which is also the Playground Teacher, and move around the outside squares by rolling a dice. Players enter the Playground (centre of the board) when they land on Entrance Squares with arrows. Calm Cards are collected to get out of 'Trouble' free. When players land on 'Trouble' squares, they move to whichever corner square they are sent to, unless they have a Calm Card. Players collect Awards as they land on them. Awards are read out and presented with congratulations and a handshake. If a player lands on an Award that has already been won, the Award is presented to the new winner with a handshake and congratulations. Keep things balanced between talking about the teaching points and playing the game. Sprinkle liberally with verbal reinforcers, for example, 'Thank you for waiting' (sharing, using manners, telling us that). Respectfully help children resolve any problems that arise. Hand out small 'prizes' at the end, for example, stickers, lollies, pipe-cleaners, plasticine, lucky dips, badges, pens. Smile lots and have fun.

Playground

Equipment

- ▸ Game Board (CD)
- ▸ Calm Cards (CD)
- ▸ Awards (CD)
- ▸ Dice or Spinner (CD)
- ▸ Counters
- ▸ Incentives

Rules

The aim is to get into the Playground and collect as many Awards as you can. Start on GO, which is also the Playground Teacher. Throw the dice and move around the outside of the board until you enter the Playground.

Squares

- ▸ **Entrance:** Follow the directions on the 6 corner squares with arrows to get into the Playground.

- ▸ **Calm Card:** Read the Calm Card aloud and keep it to get out of trouble free. After it is used to get out of Trouble, return it to the pack.

- ▸ **Headteacher's Office:** Move to this square when sent there, unless you have a Calm Card. Get out by rolling a 6 or paying £50. Visitors roll again.

- ▸ **Chill Out Zone:** Move to this square when sent there unless you have a Calm Card. Take a deep breath and chill out. Visitors roll again.

- ▸ **Suspension:** Miss a turn if you are sent there unless you have a Calm Card. Visitors roll again.

- ▸ **Playground Teacher:** Move to this square when sent there unless you have a Calm Card. Visitors roll again.

- ▸ **Stand up Tall:** Stand assertively with head up, shoulders back, looking ahead.

- ▸ **Awards:** When someone lands on an Award, it is presented to him or her with congratulations and a hand shake. If the Award has already been won, that player presents the Award to the new winner.

Continue until all the Awards have been won.

Have Fun!

Paying Compliments and Group Cohesion

Give Me Strength

'Give Me Strength' is a non-competitive game with wide appeal, including adults. The game includes fun and friendly actions like giving a compliment, waiting for others, talking about feelings, being kind and working together. Winning is not the object of the game and the game ends with everyone finishing together. Strength Cards have positive qualities written on them and are given to each other. There is a chance to talk about feelings when players land on Pick a Face squares. 'Give Me Strength' is a great game to play for group unity, as well as just for the fun of it.

Before starting

Work out some basic rules, like listening to each other, waiting for your turn, and saying nice things. If necessary, identify emotional first-aid strategies for anyone who gets upset while playing. Spend time talking about the game and the main teaching points before starting. Keep things balanced between talking and playing. Make up 'scripts' or short sayings from the following teaching points to use during the game:

▸ Looking for strengths in each other encourages us.

▸ Co-operation helps us get along together.

▸ We are all strong in different ways.

▸ Trust is important when we talk about our feelings.

▸ Winning is not the most important thing in a game – trying our best and having fun are.

▸ We can be kind to people who are not our friends and include them in our games.

How to play

Play the game in groups of more than three and up to six children. Players move around the board by rolling a dice and following the instructions on the squares. Game leaders read out the 'Strength Cards' and 'Face Cards' if necessary. The game is over when everyone gets to the finish. Sprinkle liberally with comments like, 'Thank you for waiting' (sharing, using manners, telling us that, listening, sitting still). Respectfully help children resolve any problems that arise. Hand out incentives or small prizes at the end of the game, for example, stickers, lollies, pipe-cleaners, plasticine, lucky dips, badges. Smile lots and have fun.

Give Me Strength

Equipment

- Game Board (CD)
- Strength Cards (CD)
- Counters
- Dice or Spinner (CD)
- Face Cards (CD)

Rules

The aim is to gain as much STRENGTH as you can. Roll the dice, move around the board and follow the instructions.

Squares

- **Strength Card:** Pick up a Strength Card. Read it aloud. Give it to the person in the game who is like this.

- **Pick a Face:** Pick up a Face Card and tell about a time when you felt like this.

- **Swap Places:** Swap your game-place with the person on your right. Pick up some Strength.

- **Kind/Strength:** Tell about something kind you have done or about one of your strengths. Pick up some Strength.

- **Catch Up:** Move the counter of the person who is coming last to your square. Pick up some Strength.

- **All in Together:** When a player lands on this square, all players move to this square.

- **Finish:** Wait for your friends or join the person coming last and keep playing.

Continue until everyone reaches the end.

Have Fun!

Meeting Challenges

Strong and Smart

'Strong and Smart' is designed to help children aged 9 to 14 consider the strengths they bring to solving problems. 'Challenges' deal with unfairness, hard work and restitution, and cover school, peer, family and physical areas of life. Strong Cards explore values, emotional control and the importance of physical wellbeing. Smart Cards suggest helpful strategies like setting goals, positive self talk, getting organised and focusing attention. The Aboriginal story of the Rainbow Serpent is the inspiration for this game.

Before starting

Work out some basic rules, like listening to each other, waiting for your turn, and saying nice things. If necessary, identify emotional first-aid strategies for anyone who gets upset while playing. Cover the main teaching points while explaining the game and looking through the Strong and Smart cards. Choose Challenges suitable to the age of the players and add your own challenges. Make up 'scripts' or short sayings from the following teaching points to use during the game:

1. We can meet challenges when we stop and think about solving the problem.

2. We are strong when we stay calm, walk away from trouble, do our best, don't give in, keep fit, healthy.

3. We are smart when we decide if we can ignore something, ask to talk, tell ourselves to take it if we get out in games, tell someone to stop being unfair, say sorry, offer to fix our mistakes, ask for help, make a plan, concentrate.

4. It's strong and smart to say, 'No' to our friends if they have a bad idea.

5. It's strong and smart to say, 'Stop it' if someone is being unfair to us.

How to play the game

Play in groups of up to six children. Players start on the Rainbow Serpent's head with a Challenge of their choice and move around the board by rolling the dice. Players collect Strong and Smart cards that meet their Challenge. Leaders read the cards aloud if necessary and ask if the idea will help meet the challenge. When players have both a Strong and Smart card that meets their Challenge, they call 'Challenge' and present their ideas. Strong and Smart cards are returned, Challenge cards kept and a new Challenge chosen. Not every card will meet every challenge. Players swap cards when someone lands on 'Swap'. Keep a balance between talking and playing the game. Sprinkle liberally with verbal reinforcers like, 'Thank you for waiting' (sharing, using manners, telling us that, listening, sitting still). Respectfully help children solve any problems that arise. Hand out incentives or small prizes at the end of the game, for example, stickers, lollies, coloured pipe-cleaners, plasticine, coins, lucky dips, badges. Smile lots and have fun.

Strong and Smart

Equipment

- ▸ Game Board (CD)
- ▸ Strong Cards (CD)
- ▸ Dice or Spinner (CD)
- ▸ Incentives
- ▸ Challenges (CD)
- ▸ Smart Cards (CD)
- ▸ Counters

Rules

The aim is to win as many Challenges as you can by collecting Strong and Smart cards that meet your Challenge.

- ▸ Start on the Rainbow Serpent's head with a Challenge of your choice. Roll the dice and move around the Rainbow Serpent collecting cards as you go.

- ▸ **Challenges:** Players choose a Physical, School, Friendship or Family Challenge. Challenges are met by collecting both a Strong and Smart idea to solve the problem. Players call 'Challenge' when they have a Strong and Smart card and explain how these ideas meet the Challenge. Strong and Smart cards are returned to the pack and a new Challenge chosen.

- ▸ **Strong cards:** Strong cards are read aloud. Players decide if the idea will meet their Challenge. If not, keep it to swap.

- ▸ **Smart cards:** Smart cards are read aloud. Players decide if the idea will help meet their Challenge. If not, keep it to swap.

- ▸ **Swap:** When anyone lands on Swap, everyone has a chance to swap Strong and Smart cards with each other.

- ▸ **Serpent's Head:** Players roll again.

- ▸ Continue until you are out of time or Challenges.

Have Fun!

Bibliography

Bandura, A. (1986) *Social Foundations of Thought and Action: A Social Cognitive Theory*, Englewood Cliffs, NJ: Prentice-Hall.

Blum, R. (2000) *Healthy Youth Development: A Resiliency Paradigm for Adolescent Health Development, 3rd pacific Rim Conference of the International Association for Adolescent Health:* Lincoln University, Christchurch, June.

Butler, K. (1997) The anatomy of resilience. *Family Therapy Networks*, March/April, 22-31.

Connolly, J. A., Doyle, A. B. & Reznick, E. (1988). Social pretend play and social interactions in preschoolers. *Journal of Applied Developmental Psychology*, 9, 301-313.

Dromi, G. P. & Krampf, Z. (1986). *Programming revisited: The Miftan Experience.* Social Work with Groups, 9, 91-105.

Fromberg, D. P. (1992). A review of research on play. In C. Seefeldt (Ed), *The early childhood curriculum:* A review of current research (2nd ed.). New York: Teachers College Press.

Hawley, D. R. & DeHaan, L. (1996) *Toward a definition of family resilience: Integrating life-span and family perspectives.* Family Processes, 35(3), 283-298.

Malouff, J. & Schutte, N. (1998). *Games to enhance Social and Emotional Skills: Sixty-Six Games that Teach Children, Adolescents and Adults Skills Crucial to Success in Life.* Hares C. Thomas, Publisher, Ltd., Springfield Illinois.

Pert, C. B., (1999). *Molecules of Emotion: The Science Behind Mind-Body Medicine.* New York: Touchstone, Simon and Schuster.

Porter, D. B. (1995). *Computer games: Paradigms of opportunity. Behavior Research Methods*, Instruments and Computers, 27, 229-234.

Redl, F. (1966) *When We Deal With Children*, The Free Press, New York.

Schaefli, A., Rest, J. R. & Thoma, S. J. (1985). Does moral education improve moral judgement? A meta-analysis of intervention studies using the defining issues test. *Review of Educational Research*, 55, 319-352.

Sheridan, M. K., Foley, G. M. & Radlinski, S. H. (1995). *Using Supportive Play Model: Individualised Intervention in Early Childhood Practice.* Teachers College Press, New York, London.

Smilansky, S. & Shefatya, L. (1990). *Facilitating play: A medium for promoting cognitive, socio-emotional and academic development in young children.* Gaithersburg, MD: Psychosocial & Educational Publications.

Vygotsky, L. S. (1962) *Thought and Language*, Cambridge, Mass: MIT Press.

Vygotsky, L. S. (1976) 'Play and its role in the mental development of the child'. In J. S. Bruner, A. Jolly, & K. Sylvia (eds) *Play – Its role in development and evolution*, pp 537-554. New York: Basic Books.

Walsh, F. (1996) *The concept of family resilience: Crisis and Challenge Family Processes*, 35(3) 261-281

Wood, M. & Long, N. (1991) *Life Space Intervention*, PRO-ED, Austen, Texas.

Printed and bound by CPI Group (UK) Ltd, Croydon, CR0 4YY